extreme threats

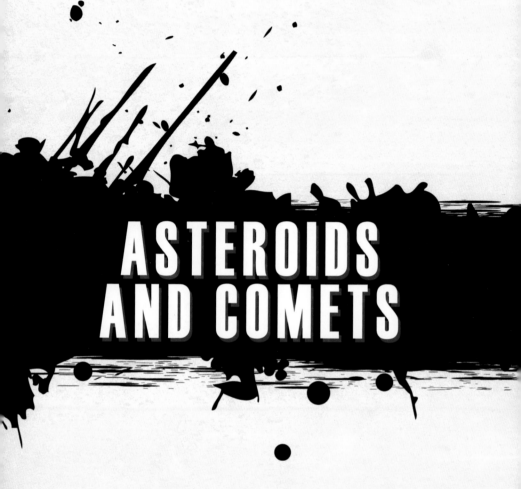

ASTEROIDS AND COMETS

extreme threats

ASTEROIDS AND COMETS

Don Nardo

MORGAN
REYNOLDS
PUBLISHING

Greensboro, NC

Designed and produced by OTTN Publishing, Stockton, N.J.

Morgan Reynolds Publishing
620 South Elm Street, Suite 387
Greensboro, NC 27406
www.morganreynolds.com
1-800-535-1504

First printing

1 3 5 7 9 8 6 4 2

Library of Congress Cataloging-in-Publication Data

  Nardo, Don, 1947-
   Asteroids and comets / by Don Nardo.
      p. cm. – (Extreme threats)
   Includes bibliographical references and index.
   ISBN 978-1-59935-121-6 (alk. paper)
   1. Asteroids–Collisions with Earth–Juvenile literature. 2.
  Comets–Collisions with Earth–Juvenile literature. I. Title.
   QB377.N37 2009
   523.44–dc22
                                                    2009026295

extreme threats

ASTEROIDS AND COMETS   **VOLCANOES**
CLIMATE CHANGE   **WILDFIRES**

TABLE OF CONTENTS

Asteroids and comets with orbits that pass through the inner solar system are known as near-Earth objects (NEOs). Scientists have identified about 170 NEOs so far, and believe that there may be thousands of other objects that could, at the very least, cause severe damage; in a worst-case scenario, collision with a large asteroid or comet could wipe out nearly all life on Earth.

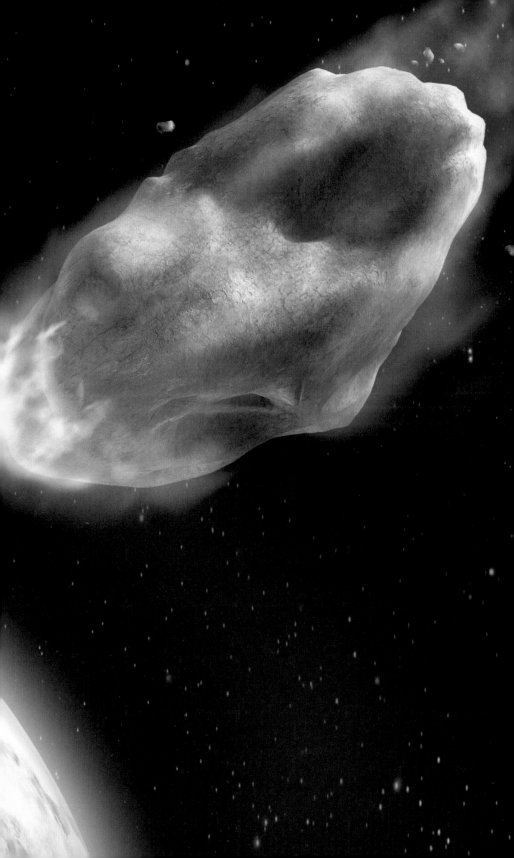

chapter one

The Day the Sky Exploded

It was exceedingly fortunate for humanity that the catastrophe of June 30, 1908, occurred in a remote, sparsely populated section of Siberia, in east-central Russia. "If it had struck a highly populated area," one modern expert remarked, "the deaths would have numbered in the millions, and the injuries even more." Because the incident took place near the Tunguska River, it became known as the Tunguska event (or Tunguska blast). It consisted of a blinding flash of light, followed by a huge explosion that destroyed many square miles of dense forest.

Although few people lived in that part of Siberia, several individuals did witness the event from various distances. Their accounts, gathered in the years following the blast, have survived. These reports have helped scientists piece together a credible explanation for one of the most spectacular natural disasters of modern times.

This map shows the approximate location of the 1908 Tunguska event within Russia. The powerful explosion occurred in the vast, sparsely populated region known as Siberia.

"I Felt a Great Heat"

The closest humans to the explosion were some animal herders camped in tents about 19 miles (30 km) away. One of them later recalled:

> Early in the morning when everyone was asleep in the tent, it was blown up in the air along with its occupants. Some lost consciousness. When they regained consciousness, they heard a great deal of noise and saw the forest burning around them, much of it devastated. The ground shook and an incredibly prolonged roaring was heard. Everything round about was shrouded in smoke and fog from burning, falling trees. Eventually the noise died away and the wind

dropped, but the forest went on burning. Many reindeer rushed away and were lost.

The blast lifted another man in the area some forty feet
off the ground and smashed him into a tree, badly shatter-
ing his arm. Meanwhile, the mighty shock wave generated
by the explosion continued to move outward. Some people, situated about 37 miles (60 km) away, said it was so
forceful that it threw them to the ground as if they were rag
dolls. An eyewitness located 66 miles (106 km) from the
blast site had a similar experience:

> I was sitting on the porch of the house at the trad-
> ing station, looking north. Suddenly in the north
> . . . the sky was split in two, and high above the for-
> est the whole northern part of the sky appeared cov-
> ered with fire. I felt a great heat, as if my shirt had
> caught fire. . . . At that moment there was a bang in
> the sky, and a mighty crash . . . I was thrown twen-
> ty feet from the porch and lost consciousness for a
> moment. . . . The crash was followed by a noise like
> stones falling from the sky, or guns firing. The earth
> trembled. . . . At the moment when the sky opened,
> a hot wind, as if from a cannon, blew past the huts
> from the north. It damaged the onion plants. Later,
> we found that many panes in the windows had been
> blown out and the iron hasp in the barn door had
> been broken.

Another distant observer reported:

> I saw the sky in the north open to the ground and fire
> poured out. The fire was brighter than the sun. We were
> terrified, but the sky closed again and immediately
> afterward, bangs like gunshots were heard. We thought
> stones were falling. . . . I ran with my head down and
> covered, because I was afraid stones may fall on it.

Entire Forests Flattened

A Siberian resident named Akulina Lyuchetkana later gave investigators a vivid description of the way the Tunguska blast devastated miles of forest:

The whirlwind knocked the *dyukcha* [wooden framework of her hut] down on me and a pole injured my leg. I crawled out from under the poles and wept. . . . I look upon our forest and don't see it. Many of the trees are standing there without branches, without leaves. Many, many trees are lying on the ground. On the ground the dry tree-trunks, the twigs, the reindeer moss are all burning. I see some sort of clothes burning. I come closer and see our rabbit-fur blanket and our fur bag, in which Ivan and I were sleeping. . . . The fire began to diminish. In place of the heat, it grew cold. We decided to move toward the Katanga [river]. By the time we got to the Chambe river . . . all around we saw marvels, terrible marvels. It wasn't our forest [anymore]. I never saw a forest like that. It was strange somehow. Where we lived there had been dense forest, an old forest. But now in many places there was no forest at all. On the mountains all the trees lay flat, and it was bright, and everything was visible for a far distance. And below the mountains in the swamps it was impossible to go at all. Some trees were standing, some were lying, some were leaning, some had fallen on one another. Many trees were scorched, [and] the needles and moss were still burning and smoking.

The Strangeness of the Evidence

A number of witnesses also reported that a giant mushroom-shaped cloud rose high into the sky from the place where the explosion had occurred. No one compared it to a nuclear mushroom cloud. At that point in time, humanity's first nuclear blast lay thirty-seven years in the future. Similarly, none of the eyewitness accounts of the

This photograph taken during Leonid Kulik's expedition to Siberia shows trees strewn across the countryside near Tunguska, Russia. The 1908 blast, probably caused by a meteorite, leveled everything for miles around the impact site.

Tunguska event were gathered until many years later. This was because neither scientists nor anyone else investigated the blast site right after the explosion. On the one hand, the area was extremely remote and difficult to reach. On the other, the turmoil created by World War I, the Russian Revolution, and other political and social upheavals affecting Russia long made mounting a major expedition impractical.

It was not until 1921—thirteen years after the event—that Russian scientist Leonid Kulik first surveyed the Tunguska region. Seeing some of the widespread devastation, he theorized that a large meteor, a hunk of rock from outer space, had struck the area. Kulik realized that the scope of the disaster warranted a major study, and he persuaded the Soviet government to send a full-scale expedition. Yet six more years elapsed before the scientific team, headed by Kulik himself, was able to make it to the site.

The researchers were immediately astounded by the scope of the destruction. The forests were almost completely flattened for a distance of 30 miles (50 km) in all directions from ground zero, a total of 830 square miles (2,150 sq. km). In most cases, the tree trunks had been largely stripped of their bark. The scientists estimated that a total of at least 80 million trees had been ruined.

The major exception was in the center of the blast zone, where a few trees were still standing. The investigators found this extremely odd, partly because in that spot they had expected to find a large crater gouged out by the meteor's impact. But lengthy searches of the entire region revealed no crater. In the years that followed, the meteor impact theory remained the chief explanation for the event. But the lack of a crater, coupled with the mystery of the trees still standing in the center of the disaster area, continued to baffle researchers.

In part because of the strangeness of some of the evidence, some scientists and writers later proposed other explanations for the Tunguska explosion. One theory suggested that a big pocket of natural gas located under the area had suddenly exploded. Other researchers speculated that a small piece of antimatter had fallen into Earth's atmosphere, causing a huge blast. (An exotic material that is rare in the universe, antimatter supposedly explodes violently when it comes into contact with ordinary matter.)

Russian engineer and writer Alexander Kazantsev advanced an even more outlandish idea in 1946. He had studied the nuclear blast that the U.S. military had detonated at Hiroshima, Japan, the year before and had noticed strong similarities to the Tunguska event. He realized that back in 1908 humans had yet to discover nuclear energy. So he proposed that an alien spaceship had accidentally exploded over Siberia, unleashing nuclear devastation. (This concept was also explored by drama critics John Baxter and Thomas Atkins in their 1976 book *The Fire Came By*.)

A Large Air Blast

As it turned out, the similarities between Tunguska and Hiroshima were highly instructive in determining the cause of the 1908 blast. But there was no need to invoke alien visitation or other far-fetched hypotheses. In the 1950s and 1960s, further studies of the Tunguska area revealed tiny particles of iron and nickel imbedded in the

Eyewitnesses to the Tunguska event said they saw a mushroom cloud rising over the explosion site—similar to the one that appeared when a nuclear bomb was detonated over the Japanese city of Hiroshima in August 1945.

fallen tree trunks. This finding was consistent with the explosion of a meteor or small asteroid, objects having high concentrations of these metals.

Scientists also noted that the Hiroshima blast and other nuclear explosions had not formed craters because they had been detonated thousands of feet above the ground. Further calculations showed that the Tunguska meteor's explosion was also an airblast. About 100 to 200 feet (30 to 60 m) across and traveling at 9 miles (15 km) per second, it had blown to bits about 3 to 6 miles (5 to 10 km) above Earth's surface. This created a large blast wave. As it expanded outward, it struck the trees directly beneath it vertically—that is, in the same direction as their upright trunks, so they remained standing. But the blast delivered a more horizontal blow to the trees located outside of ground zero, thereby flattening them.

Lessons from Tunguska

The Tunguska event taught scientists much more than the mechanics of extraterrestrial objects exploding in the atmosphere. (The term *terrestrial* denotes things that exist on Earth; so *extraterrestrial* refers to things that originate or occur beyond Earth, in outer space.) Some researchers pointed out that the disaster could have been far worse. If the meteor had entered the atmosphere only a few hours later than it did, it would have struck one of Russia's major cities, St. Petersburg. More than a million people would have perished in an instant.

Others say that the remoteness of the Siberian blast site was not the only piece of good luck associated with the

A Strong Mechanical Shock

Noted planetary scientist William K. Hartmann explained what happens when an object like the Tunguska meteor explodes in the atmosphere:

> Because the meteor did not strike the ground or make a crater, early researchers thought the object might be a weak, icy fragment of a comet, which vaporized explosively in the air, and left no residue on the ground. However, modern planetary scientists have much better tools for understanding meteor explosions in the atmosphere. As a meteor slams into the atmosphere at speeds around 12 to 20 km/sec or more, it experiences a strong mechanical shock, like a diver belly-flopping into water. This can break apart stones of a certain size range, which explode instead of hitting the ground. Some of them drop brick-sized fragments on the ground, but others, such as the one that hit Siberia, may produce primarily a fireball and cloud of fine dust and tiny fragments. In 1993 researchers Chris Chyba, Paul Thomas, and Kevin Zahnle studied the Siberian explosion and concluded it was of this type—a stone meteor that exploded in the atmosphere. This conclusion was supported when Russian researchers found tiny stony particles embedded in the trees at the collision site, matching the composition of common stone meteorites.

onrushing Tunguska meteor. The fact that it blew up over land was also fortunate. If the same object had exploded in one of the planet's many oceans, it would have created large sea waves. Scientists call such a wave a tsunami, from

A scientist holds a small case containing tiny metal spherules found at Tunguska. The shape and composition of the particles indicate that a meteorite exploded over the area in 1908.

Japanese words meaning "harbor wave." University of Arizona scientist John S. Lewis explained the consequences of such a sea strike:

> The seabed is cracked by the blast wave, melted, and scoured by the one-hundred-thousand-degree fireball. Hundreds of cubic kilometers of water are vaporized [and] when the surface of the fireball coasts to a stop in the water, the ocean surface collapses back into the cavity. . . . As the wave crest approaches the center of the crater, fast-moving waves converging from all directions pile into each other, rushing headlong into a monstrous surge that shoots up a towering pillar of water higher than the highest mountains on Earth. The sea sloshes back and forth in the blast region, pumping the

surrounding ocean and generating circular wave fronts which, like the ripples from a pebble tossed into a puddle, spread out in all directions.

Such waves would devastate nearby coastlines, crushing and drowning hundreds of thousands of people. More frightening still is the realization that the Tunguska object was tiny in comparison to some of the meteors, asteroids, and comets that are at this moment hurtling through nearby parts of our solar system. Objects millions of times more massive than the Tunguska meteor have struck Earth in the past, with terrifying results. It is 100 percent certain that they will do so again in the future. And therein lies the gripping story of the largest, most destructive threat the human race presently faces.

chapter Two

Evidence for Deadly Impacts

The Barringer Meteor Crater is a gigantic hole in the arid Arizona desert. The crater is nearly three-quarters of a mile (1.2 km) wide and 570 feet (180 m) deep; the rim of the crater rises another 150 feet (45 m) above the surrounding sandstone desert.

M ost people have never given much, if any, thought to the odds of their dying in an extraterrestrial impact event. At first glance, the likelihood of a comet or asteroid striking a given town certainly seems quite small. One researcher who has calculated the odds of dying by various accidental causes suggests that there is only one chance in ten thousand of being killed by such an impact. That is a hundred times less likely than dying in a car crash, which itself has odds of one in a hundred. Dying in an impact is also less likely than dying in an accidental shooting (with odds of one in 2,500). However, many people are surprised to learn that the chance of being killed by a comet or asteroid is actually higher than of dying in an airplane crash (one in 20,000). It is also higher than the chance of dying in a tornado (one in 60,000).

Because the vast majority of people are unaware of such estimates, they have little or no immediate fear of extraterrestrial impacts. But large numbers of people are afraid to fly in planes, even though the risk of death from plane crashes is lower than from impacts. "If people reacted to the impact threat [as] many do to flying," space researcher Duncan Steel pointed out

> the coasts would be deserted for miles inland [out of fear of impact-generated tsunamis], and all would have fled to the high country [with] fingers crossed that the impact is not too nearby. The actual hazard does not warrant such steps, but it does warrant a much greater [safety] effort than is being applied at present. Humankind may expect between 5,000 and 10,000 people per [year] to die due to impacts, averaged over many years, with a small but finite chance that billions may be killed one year soon.

In other words, like crashes of jumbo jets, impact events happen fairly infrequently. But when they do happen, large numbers of people might die.

Two Main Kinds of Impactor

Scientists now know that the probability of such impacts depends on a number of different factors. Duncan Steel compared an asteroid or comet hitting Earth with several blindfolded people moving around in a room:

> All of the people in the room are moving around in random directions at different speeds. You want to know the probability that one will collide with you. Obviously, the more people in the room, the higher

the probability of a collision. Also, if the room is small, more collisions will occur, whereas if it is vast, collisions are less frequent. [In addition] if everyone stands still, the probability of collision equals zero, whereas if everyone is moving quickly, the probability of a collision becomes large. [Finally] if you are fat, you present a large target and a collision is more likely, whereas if you are thin, you are a smaller target and the probability of collision is smaller.

Similarly, if many objects are moving through space near Earth and the moon, the probability of an impact is higher than if few objects are in the area. And Earth, which is a much larger target than the moon, can be expected to suffer more impacts than the smaller body.

The comet Hale-Bopp was photographed in the constellation Andromeda, March 1997, when the comet was making its closest approach to the Sun. As a comet nears the inner solar system, heat from the Sun vaporizes some of the ice on its surface, creating a long tail composed of dust and ions charged with electricity.

Another important factor in such impacts is the nature of the impacting object, or impactor. The two principal kinds of impactor that pose a threat to Earth and humanity are comets and asteroids. Each is physically distinct and formed in a different manner. A comet is essentially what scientists have colorfully come to call a "dirty snowball" drifting through space. According to astronomer Patricia Barnes-Svarney:

> At great distances from the sun, the comet's nucleus [its solid part], consisting of mostly water ice, ammonia, carbon dioxide, and other exotic compounds, remains inert [inactive]. It is when the body ventures toward the inner solar system that heat from the sun begins to warm the ices and snows of the "dirty snowball," causing them to vaporize (evaporate). . . . Pushed by the solar wind away from the sun is a distinct tail of dust and [gases] streaming from the comet's head at speeds of hundreds of meters per second.

The nuclei of comets vary in size from a few hundred feet to several miles across. The second major kind of impactor, an asteroid, is a hunk of rock (or a mixture of rock and various metals) that lacks ices and gases. Asteroids range in size from a few feet to many miles in diameter. Scientists usually refer to asteroids smaller than about 30 feet across as meteors, or meteoroids. One that survives a fall through the atmosphere is called a meteorite.

Two Different Ancient Scenarios

The main reason that comets and asteroids are physically different is that they formed in different ways. About 4.5

billion years ago, when the solar system was young, trillions of objects of various sizes swirled around the infant sun. Astronomers call them planetesimals. Over time, gravity compelled many of these objects to clump together. And in this way larger objects, including the planets and their moons, formed.

Most of the planetsimals near the sun ended up becoming part of the inner, rocky planets—Mercury, Venus, Earth, and Mars. But farther out, beyond Mars, a different ancient scenario played out. The huge gravity of the giant planet Jupiter relentlessly pulled and pushed on many of the outer planetesimals, keeping them from coming together to form planets. So they remained separate, and continued to orbit the sun in the so-called asteroid belt, which lies between Mars and Jupiter.

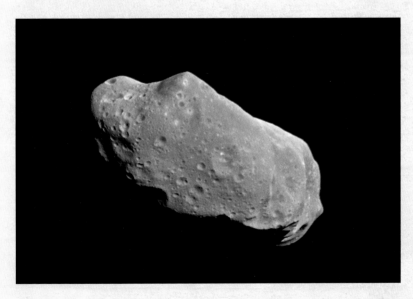

This NASA photograph of a large asteroid—more than 35 miles (56 km) long—shows many craters, evidence of numerous collisions with other rocky materials drifting in space. When asteroids collide, broken pieces are sometimes sent rocketing toward Earth and other planets of the inner solar system.

Some of the asteroids in the belt collided with one another, creating smaller objects. Others strayed too close to Jupiter, whose gravity yanked them out of the belt. Of the separated bodies, some floated into the inner solar system, where they collided with Earth and other inner planets. Others escaped the solar system and disappeared into the inky black voids lying between the stars. Still others ended up in another ring of orbiting objects lying beyond Neptune's orbit–the Kuiper Belt.

Pinball on a Planetary Scale

The well-known Canadian astronomer David H. Levy called the Oort Cloud "the result of a long game of interplanetary pinball." He added:

The youthful solar system was filled with comets—in Earth's primordial [early] sky there must have been dozens of bright comets at a time. Some of the comets collided with the planets. Others made close passes by the planets, using their gravity to swing off into new orbits that would eventually land them near other planets. As the largest planet, Jupiter was the clear winner in this game. A comet swinging by Jupiter would get a gravitational hurl that would send the comet either out of the solar system forever, or off into the growing Oort Cloud. Within about 500 million years of the solar system's birth, the pinball game was all but over, its supply of cometary materials exhausted. . . . The process continues even today, but at a far more leisurely rate.

Meanwhile, the inner solar system was too hot for frozen gases and ices to survive. So these materials drifted outward toward the giant planets–Jupiter, Saturn, Uranus, and Neptune. Untold millions or even billions of icy planetesimals formed near these large bodies, whose gravities then hurled them still farther out.

The exiled bodies banded together into a vast cloud of comets that hovered well beyond the Kuiper Belt in the solar system's dark, cold outer reaches. Scientists named it the Oort Cloud after Dutch astronomer Jan Oort, who in the 1940s correctly predicted its existence. Not all of these objects remain there, however. Various factors, including cometary collisions, cause some of them to travel inward toward the sun, where they grow gaseous tails and become visible to people on Earth. On occasion, these wayward travelers wander too close to our planet and, guided by gravity's invisible hand, strike it.

Rise of the Impact Theory

Earth was in the past, and remains today, under the threat of periodic bombardment from asteroids and comets. It is important to emphasize that most scientists did not recognize this threat until fairly recently. The first major researcher to suggest that extraterrestrial impacts play a major role in shaping the planet was the eighteenth-century English astronomer Edmond Halley. He is most famous for his discovery that the bright comets that had appeared in 1451, 1531, 1607, and 1682 were all one and the same object. After his death in 1742, his colleagues named it Halley's Comet in his honor.

Less well known is the fact that Halley proposed that comets sometimes crash into Earth. In 1694, he suggested that the great flood described in the Bible might have been caused by such an impact. Two years later, another English researcher, William Whiston, published a book that explored the notion of large impact events shaping history.

One reason that these ideas did not catch on was that church leaders opposed them. In their view, suggestions that natural forces caused biblical events was unacceptable, because they cast doubt on God's role in such events. Also, most scientists thought that the impact theory was too far-fetched. Not until the twentieth century did serious attempts to resurrect that theory take place. One was initiated by American astronomers Fletcher Watson and Ralph Baldwin. In 1941, they studied three recently discovered asteroids that passed fairly close to Earth and proposed that large impact events might be more common than previously thought.

The Galileo spacecraft took these images of the moon in 1992; the distinct crater within the bright area at the bottom of the image is the enormous Tycho crater, which is more than 50 miles (85 km) across. The dark areas are impact basins filled with lava rock: Oceanus Procellarum (on the left), Mare Imbrium (center left), Mare Serenitatis and Mare Tranquillitatis (center), and Mare Crisium (near the right edge).

The response from most scientists was: if impacts are common in history, where are the craters? Baldwin offered a partial answer in his 1949 book *The Face of the Moon*. In it, he argued that most of the thousands of craters on the moon's surface were caused by impacts. Referring to one of the more prominent of these, Tycho Crater, Baldwin said: "The explosion that caused the crater Tycho would, anywhere on Earth, be a horrifying thing, almost inconceivable in its monstrosity."

However, most researchers had long assumed that the lunar craters were the result of volcanic eruptions. Many continued to cling to this view. As late as 1958, a leading Russian astronomer declared, "We can now regard as completely unfounded the [view] of the origins of [lunar craters], which ascribes them to the fall of meteorites."

Terrestrial Impact Scars

Supporters of the impact theory persisted, however. As time went on they uncovered more and more evidence for it. Particularly revealing were studies of lunar rocks recovered in the Apollo moon missions of the 1960s and 1970s. These showed unmistakably that the lunar craters had been created by impact events. Scientists now realized that Earth, too, must have undergone extensive bombardment by asteroids and comets over the ages. Because Earth is more massive than the moon, it must have been struck considerably more often than its natural satellite. The difference is that the moon has no air and water. So its craters do not undergo constant erosion, and they remain visible for millions of years. In contrast, impact craters on Earth, called terrestrial craters, are steadily erased by the effects of rain, wind, tides, volcanoes, and so forth.

Scientists paid especially close attention to Barringer Crater (also called Meteor Crater), near Winslow, Arizona. It is 4,000 feet (1,200 m) wide and 570 feet (170 m) deep. Because it is relatively young–only about 50,000 years old–and also because it lies in an arid region, it has undergone minimal erosion. As a result, it looks similar to what it looked like when it formed. For more than a century, scientists thought the crater had been created by a volcanic outburst or a big steam explosion. But modern studies

Apollo 12 astronaut Charles Conrad Jr. walks down the side of a moon crater to examine a piece of scientific equipment. During the six successful Apollo moon landings (1969–1972), astronauts carefully examined the lunar surface. The rocks and soil samples they brought back to Earth proved that meteorite impacts had indeed created the moon's cratered surface.

How an Impact Crater Forms

The late, great planetary scientist Eugene M. Shoemaker and his wife, astronomer Carolyn S. Shoemaker, provided this clear-cut description of the formation of an impact crater:

> When a sizable solid body strikes the ground at high speed, shock waves [move] into the target rocks and into the impacting body. At collision speeds of tens of kilometers per second, the initial pressure on [these materials] is millions of times Earth's normal atmospheric pressure. This can squeeze even dense rock into one-third of its usual volume. Stress so overwhelms the target material that the rock initially flows almost like a fluid. [As] more and more of the target rock becomes engulfed by the shock wave, which expands more or less [sideways] away from the point of impact, [a] rapidly expanding cavity [or crater, is] created. . . . The impacting body [itself], now melted or vaporized, moves outward [and] lines the cavity walls.

showed that it had been excavated by the detonation of an impactor roughly 165 feet (50 m) across. Barnes-Svarney described the blast, which was equal to that of about 150 Hiroshima bombs:

> The impacting body was as bright as the sun and it hit with a blinding flash. Immediately after, [the] blast created a tall column of dust and debris and turned flat sedimentary beds [of rocks and earth] into crumpled and overturned outcrops, as if someone had carelessly scooped out a piece of the Earth. The noise must have been deafening. A rain of rocky debris fell

Scientists believe the enormous Barringer Meteor Crater was created approximately 50,000 years ago by the impact of a meteorite approximately 165 feet (50 m) in diameter.

back to the Earth, while the dust from the impact . . . was carried by the prevailing winds from the west.

Many other terrestrial impact craters, in various states of preservation, have been identified. Australia has several, including the relatively small Wolfe Creek Crater (about .5 miles/.8 km across), which formed about 300,000 years ago, and the much larger Lake Acraman (a dry lake bed 22 miles/35 km across), created some 600 million years ago. Canada also boasts a number of impact craters. Among them are Mistastin Lake (17 miles/27 km across), blasted out about 38 million years ago, and one of the largest impact scars on the planet, Manicouagan (62 miles/100 km across), created roughly 212 million years ago.

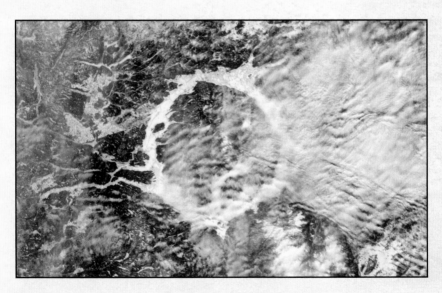

The ice-covered Manicouagin Reservoir, located in eastern Canada, marks the site of an impact crater that was once 62 miles (100 km) wide. According to geologists, this giant crater was formed 212 million years ago by a meteorite that was three miles (five km) in diameter. Over time, erosion by glaciers and weather and the deposit of river sediments have reduced the crater's visible diameter to about 45 miles (72 km).

A Cosmic String of Pearls

Because terrestrial impact craters can be examined up close, scientists have learned a great deal from studying them. However, the most numerous and in many cases vivid examples are those on other solar system bodies. The moon is only one of hundreds. Impact craters have been identified on Mercury, Mars, and many of the moons of Jupiter, Saturn, and Uranus. Such craters are even visible on asteroids, both large and small.

The reason that no impact craters are visible on the surfaces of the giant planets–Jupiter, Saturn, Uranus, and Neptune–is that the outer layers of these bodies are gaseous. So when asteroids and comets strike them, the impactors are absorbed; the scars created by the initial explosions disappear in a few days or weeks.

This fact was confirmed by one of the most spectacular natu-

This photo taken by the Mars Global Surveyor in 2006 shows an impact crater that is approximately 1.9 miles (3 km) in diameter. Toward the bottom of the image a second, more subdued circular feature can be seen; this is probably an ancient impact crater that was buried by more recent impacts—a common occurrence on Mars.

ral events ever witnessed by humans. In March 1992, noted scientists Eugene Shoemaker and David Levy discovered a new comet, which became known, appropriately, as Shoemaker-Levy 9 (because it was ninth comet this pair had found). The comet had been captured by Jupiter. A closer look confirmed that the planet's enormous gravity had torn the object apart, producing more than twenty fragments. Still traveling together, and looking like a cosmic string of pearls, they were due to strike Jupiter the following year. Between July 16 and 22, 1994, thousands of people worldwide used telescopes to witness the cometary fragments crash, one after another, into the giant planet. As John S. Lewis described it:

A 150-mile (245 km) wide crater can be seen in this photograph of the southern hemisphere of Saturn's moon Tethys, taken by the Cassini spacecraft in 2006. The peak in the center of the crater was created when it was formed.

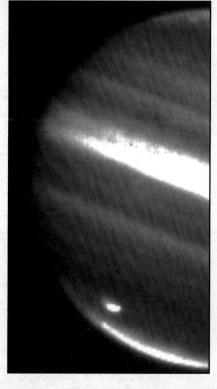

Scientists believe that Jupiter, with its strong gravitational influence, captures many small comets and asteroids that might otherwise threaten Earth and other planets of the inner solar system. (Top) This sequence of images shows a fragment from the comet Shoemaker-Levy 9 striking Jupiter in July 1994. The first image shows no impact. In the next three images, a point of light appears, flares, and then fades away, seven seconds after the first picture was taken. (Right) On July 20, 2009, NASA's Infrared Telescope Facility in Hawaii captured this image of a "scar" in Jupiter's southern hemisphere. The scar is almost as large as Earth, and scientists quickly recognized it as a sign that another comet had hit the planet.

The explosions of the larger bodies on the back side of Jupiter launched huge fireballs thousands of kilometers above the rim of the planet, into plain view from Earth. As the string of impactors dove in like runaway cars from an uncoupled train, one blast after another could be clearly seen by observers on Earth. The larger blasts left immense black smudges of dust on Jupiter's cloud-covered face. Several of the larger impact scars are much bigger than the entire surface area of Earth.

Although the exact figures are unknown, it is estimated that the largest fragments struck with the force of 10 million megatons. That is equivalent to about 500 million Hiroshima bombs. If these impactors had hit Earth rather than Jupiter, all life on our planet would have been wiped out. Among other things, the 1994 cometary impact event was a reminder that such catastrophes can cause mass extinctions. Hardly a year now passes without the discovery of more evidence that many of the documented mass extinctions in Earth's history were generated by giant impacts.

Giant Impacts and Mass Extinctions

A mass extinction is an event in which large numbers of plant and animal species are wiped out, never to return. It is one form of global catastrophe. Evidence shows clearly that many such disasters have occurred in the past, and at least some have been caused by extraterrestrial impacts. If such a catastrophe happened today or next week, it could be potentially devastating for humanity, even if many species were not destroyed.

In their classic book *Cosmic Catastrophes*, scientists Clark R. Chapman and David Morrison attempted to define a globally catastrophic impact event. At a minimum, they stated, it would kill 25 percent of the world's population outright, and/or it would ruin most of a year's worth of crops and other food needed to sustain human societies. An impact event on this scale would cause the global economy to collapse and threaten the stability of civilization for several decades, if not longer. It is possible that any given large impact event might not be minimal in scope. It might well be large enough to exterminate the human race, along with numerous other species.

Geologists and other scientists now estimate that global catastrophes produced by impact events occur on average once every 100,000 years. In terms of a typical human lifetime, which is less than 100 years, 100,000 years seems like an extremely long time. The chances that such a disaster will occur during the lifetimes of the people presently inhabiting the planet are fairly low. Nevertheless, global catastrophes, including mass extinctions, will happen again in the future. And even if humanity is fortunate enough to survive, it will be adversely affected.

The most effective way to estimate what such events will be like is to examine those that happened in the past. "We need to consider the story in the stones," as one expert put it.

> We need to evaluate what [took place] in past eons. This will inform us not only about the link between impacts and mass extinctions (and thus about how evolution proceeds), but also about the role of such impacts in controlling how the face of the Earth is shaped.

Worlds in Collision

No extraterrestrial impact event shaped Earth's face more than the one that occurred about 4.5 billion years ago. It was not just the planet's surface that was affected. The event, which scientists sometimes call "The Big Whack," also resulted in the formation of the moon.

The "Big Whack"—the impact of a planet-sized object 4.5 billion years ago—caused intense volcanic activity throughout the Earth.

At that time the moonless Earth was relatively young–only a few million years old. It was also in the last stages of frequent and massive bombardment by the swarms of planetesimals that dominated the early solar system. None of the objects that had yet struck the planet compared with this one, however. The impactor was roughly the size of the planet Mars, with a diameter about half that of Earth.

"Seeming to swell in size as it approached," astronomer Neil F. Comins wrote, "the planetesimal would have filled the entire sky just before it smashed into the Earth at twenty-five thousand miles an hour." The collision of the two worlds unleashed energies measuring in the range of thousands of trillions of megatons. Comins continued:

> The entire Earth convulsed as it absorbed the energy from the greatest trauma it had ever endured. Everywhere its surface buckled, cracked, and dissolved as the remains of the intruder sank toward the Earth's core. The site of the impact became an enormous sea of liquid rock so hot and bright that for hours it gave off more heat and light than the equivalent area on the surface of the sun.

Meanwhile, enormous quantities of the crusts of Earth and the impactor dislodged and blasted skyward. Some of this material later fell back to the ground. But large amounts escaped and went into orbit, forming a large ring of debris around Earth. Space is cold, so in the course of weeks and months the floating debris cooled. At the same time, gravity's inevitable and relentless hand went to work, causing these materials to clump together. Eventually, the clumps contracted into a large sphere, marking the official birth of Earth's only natural satellite–the moon.

If any life had existed on Earth (or on the impactor) at the time of the disaster, it was surely primitive, most likely consisting of nothing more advanced than one-celled organisms. Just as surely, the gargantuan energies released by the great impact annihilated these creatures. It is both intriguing and frightening to realize that this may not have been the only instance of primitive life forms going extinct

Apollo 15 astronaut James B. Irwin collects samples of the moon's rocks and soil. Scientific evaluation of the samples collected during the Apollo program shows that in many ways they are similar chemically to Earth rocks. This supports the hypothesis that the moon was created from parts of the Earth's mantle and crust that were blasted into space by the impact of a planet-sized object.

during the planet's early years. According to Barnes-Svarney:

> Life could have been killed off completely several times over by "superimpacts"—collisions between the Earth and miniplanets . . . left over from the birth of the solar system. These massive impacts could have vaporized the Earth's early oceans, melted the upper crust of the planet and erased any life that had started. . . . In fact, scientists Kevin Maher and David Stevenson of the California Institute of Technology once labeled it as the "impact frustration of the origin of life," in which impact after impact eradicated the fragile beginnings of life on the surface.

The K-T Event and Impact Winter

Eventually, primitive life did manage to take firm hold on Earth. Over time, one-celled organisms developed into more complex plants and animals that populated both the seas and continents. Giant extraterrestrial impacts were less common by this time, but they did happen periodically. Each time such an event occurred, large numbers of species were destroyed, in some cases radically changing the course of evolution on the planet.

The most famous of these mass extinctions was the one that killed most of the dinosaurs about 65 million years

(continued on page 46)

The mighty Tyrannosaurus Rex was among the dinosaurs and other creatures that disappeared from the fossil record around 65 million years ago. Scientists believe that the a large meteorite that struck Earth near Mexico's Yucatán Peninsula caused the Cretaceous-Tertiary (or K-T) extinction event, in which about 70 percent of the Earth's plant and animal life died out. The Chicxulub crater, caused by this impact, is more than 110 miles (180 km) in diameter.

If the Moon Did Not Exist

The formation of the moon from a gigantic impact event about 3.8 billion years ago forever altered Earth and its future in many ways. The first change happened immediately following the impact. The object that struck our planet excavated an enormous section of Earth's crust and caused large quantities of melted rock to flow across the surface. This significantly contributed to the shapes of Earth's continents and ocean basins. So if there had been no impact, the planet's geography would be different today.

Without the moon, Earth's tides—which are caused in large part by the moon's gravity—would be only about one-third as high as they are today. Over time, the moon's gravity also helped to slow our planet's rotation period, or day, from six to twenty-fours. If the moon had never formed, the day would now be roughly eight hours long. In such a situation, the sun would appear to race across the daytime sky in only three to four hours. Because Earth's rotation affects the winds, with no moon winds would constantly blow at sixty or seventy miles per hour. And in turn, hurricanes would be stronger and ocean waves would be higher, causing more severe beach erosion.

In addition, the composition of Earth's atmosphere would be different if the great impact event had not created the moon. The planet's air is presently about 78 percent nitrogen and 21 percent oxygen. But shortly after Earth formed, the atmosphere was composed mostly of carbon dioxide, nitrogen, and water vapor. The giant impactor stripped away some of the atmosphere, making it thinner. If this had not happened, carbon dioxide levels would have remained high. Earth would have been considerably hotter, and large numbers of the plants and

animals that later developed would have been physically quite different.

When sea creatures eventually crawled out onto dry land, the environment they faced would have been extremely harsh. In the high winds, animals would have needed to develop wide bodies with short legs to maintain stability. A majority would have grown thick skins or shells to make injuries from airborne sand and rocks less likely. And without a moon, nights would have been pitch black; so to hunt their prey, animals would have had to rely on an unusually keen sense of hearing.

Finally, if any intelligent beings ever evolved on the moonless Earth, they would have come to view the heavens differently than we do. There would have been no lunar calendar and no time periods called months. Moreover, they wouldn't see lunar or solar eclipses, because such events wouldn't have existed.

(continued from page 43)

before. (It used to be thought that all the dinosaurs died. However, today many scientists suggest that birds are survivors of the dinosaurian family.) Actually, the dinosaurs were not the only victims of the catastrophe, called the K-T event. Upwards of 70 percent of all plant and animal species perished.

Researchers estimate that the impactor was about 6 miles (9.6 km) in diameter and moving at least 12 miles per second. After tearing through the atmosphere in little more than an instant, it smashed into the shallow water near Mexico's eastern coast. The blast was so immense that it vaporized thousands of cubic miles of Earth's crust, excavating a crater more than a hundred miles across in

Volcanic eruptions like this one pour tons of ash and dust into the atmosphere. Massive amounts of volcanic activity caused by the trauma of an impacting object from space may have created a dust cloud around the planet 65 million years ago. This would have caused significant climate change and led to mass extinctions of both plants and animals.

mere seconds. Simultaneously, a gigantic fireball expanded outward in all directions. Nearby plants and animals that were not burnt to cinders in the fireball were crushed in a monstrous atmospheric shock wave that also traveled outward from ground zero. For a distance of at least a thousand miles from the crater, every living thing died in a matter of minutes.

Though terrible, these effects marked only the beginning of the disaster. Earthquakes many times larger than any ever experienced by humans rocked the continents, and towering tsunamis pulverized coastlines around the globe. Within hours, glowing pieces of rock from the fireball began raining down, igniting vast forest fires that swept across the landmasses. Even worse, within days the combination of dust from the initial explosion and soot from the fires began to block the life-sustaining inflow of sunlight. This set off a secondary global catastrophe that scientists have come to call "impact winter." (Similar phenomena caused by large volcanic eruptions or possible nuclear wars are called volcanic winter and nuclear winter, respectively.)

Explained astronomer Gerrit L. Verschuur:

Following the impact of 65 million years ago, the sheath of soot, dust and ash that enveloped the Earth turned day into darkest night, terminating photosynthesis entirely, and plunging the planet into a deep freeze. Plants died and animals starved. The darkness lasted for months. Many survivors of the initial impact and its immediate aftermath froze to death. . . . Only those that could burrow [underground] for shelter and food had a fair chance of surviving the catastrophe.

Other than insects and worms, mammals were the chief kinds of creatures that burrowed beneath the ground. And with their primary predators, the dinosaurs, gone, mammals flourished as never before. They overran the continents, exploding into thousands of new and in many cases larger and more sophisticated species. This momentous series of events graphically shows how a random incident, in this case a large impact, can, in a geologic instant, forever alter the course of evolution and history. As Verschuur pointed out:

> After the dinosaurs were ushered off the terrestrial stage, the scene was set to allow mammals to diversify until, 65 million years later, one of their kind, *Homo sapiens*, rose to prominence. Our species recently evolved to become conscious and clever enough to invent agriculture, technology, and science, and we have used our newly developed mental skills to uncover the secrets of nature that carry the clues to our origins, and to our future. To put this another way, if the comet that triggered the K-T event had arrived twenty minutes earlier or later, it would have missed the planet and we would not be here now, talking, reading, or writing about any of this.

Fate of the Giant Mammals

Other ancient mass extinctions have been attributed to large extraterrestrial impacts. The most recent theory of this type, proposed in 2007, suggests that an impact event in North America 12,900 years ago, in the Pleistocene era, killed off the so-called megafauna. These were large, in some cases giant, mammals, including the woolly mammoth, giant sloth, and saber-toothed cat.

This skull from a woolly mammoth was uncovered in South Dakota. Some experts believe that the impact of a meteorite or comet may have caused the extinction of these large, elephant-like creatures, which roamed North America and northern Eurasia until the end of the Pleistocene epoch.

According to this view, a small asteroid or comet struck a large glacier then covering what is now southern Canada. (This would explain why no telltale crater associated with the impact has been found; impact features in glaciers would disappear as the ice sheets moved and/or melted.) It is also possible that the impactor blew up in the air above the glacier. The disaster not only caused animal extinctions, but also devastated local groups of early American hunters, the so-called Clovis people. According to one of the theory's chief proponents, Douglas J. Kennett, of the University of Oregon:

> The destruction would have been instantaneous. People living in the immediate vicinity of impact or airbursts would pretty much have been annihilated. And where the impacts and airbursts would have occurred, there would have been a lot of debris kicked up into the atmosphere. . . . Also, the wildfires triggered by all this would have put smoke and soot up into the atmosphere that would also have had major atmospheric effects in terms of obscuring the sun for fairly long periods of time.

That the Pleistocene extinctions were caused by an impact event has not yet been conclusively proven. But scientists no longer view such an idea as far-fetched, as they would have a half-century ago. Mounting evidence shows that impacts of various sizes have occurred frequently throughout human history. In addition, several near misses, including some recent ones, have put humanity on notice that mass death could rain down from the skies at any time.

chapter Four

Recent Strikes and Near Misses

S tatistically speaking, a mass extinction or global catastrophe is not likely to occur next week or next year. It may be many centuries, or even tens of thousands of years, before humanity faces such an extreme threat. It has been estimated that asteroids or comets .6 miles (1 km) across hit Earth about once every 100,000 years. Objects 3 miles (5 km) across strike about once every 10 to 30 million years. It might seem, therefore, that there is little cause for worry.

Yet some sobering facts make a complete sigh of relief premature. The fact is that towns, cities, and other aspects of modern human civilization are far from immune to lesser but still devastating impact hazards. A conservative estimate places the chances of an Earth strike by an object 165 feet (50 m) across at about once per century. Remember that this was the size of the impactor that created Arizona's Barringer Crater, which unleashed energy equivalent to 150 Hiroshima bombs.

A tiny meteorite leaves a colorful streak as it flashes through the sky over Japan. Most of the space debris that reaches Earth burns up in the atmosphere before striking the planet.

A High Destructive Potential

Even more disturbing, in 1993 Eugene Shoemaker calculated the odds of encounters with somewhat smaller objects. He estimated that an impactor 33 feet (10 m) in diameter explodes on Earth or in its atmosphere at least once a year. Such a house-sized object may at first glance appear too small to do any serious damage. But as Shoemaker and others have pointed out, these objects are traveling at supersonic speeds. Most of the energy of that vigorous motion is converted into explosive force during the impact, and an impactor 33 feet across packs the explosive energy of 20,000 tons (20 kilotons) of TNT. In comparison, the blast that leveled Hiroshima in 1945 had a force of 15,000 tons, or 15 kilotons, of TNT.

Not all of these Hiroshima-size or larger explosions occur on the ground, of course. Because three-fourths of Earth's surface is covered by water, a majority of the impacting objects head toward the oceans. An object that struck the Pacific Ocean in 1994, for example, exploded with the force of almost twenty Hiroshima bombs. Fortunately, no islands or ships were near the blast site.

Also, as Shoemaker pointed out, a great many impactors detonate in the atmosphere, as the 1908 Tunguska object did. One such airblast, for instance, took place over Pennsylvania on May 4, 1945, as reported in the *New York Times*:

> Hundreds of thousands of persons in eastern Pennsylvania, New Jersey, Maryland, and Delaware were awakened early today by a blue-white flash and a series of explosions and tremors. The light streaked across the sky at 3:38 A.M. and the subsequent detonations shook houses, rattled windows, burst open doors, and sent thousands of startled persons rushing to telephones with a deluge [flood] of inquiries. . . . Most of those who actually observed the phenomenon described [it] as a major explosion.

This object was likely smaller than the one that caused the Tunguska disaster, so its destructive potential was also smaller. Still, had the Pennsylvania impactor continued on and hit the ground, it might well have demolished an entire suburban neighborhood or several city blocks. Much more ominous is the fact that a number of extraterrestrial objects as big or bigger than the Tunguska impactor have exploded high in Earth's atmosphere in recent years. Several others, including some with enormous destructive potential, have nearly missed our planet.

The passage of only a few seconds or the movement of only a few miles, more or less, kept these objects from connecting with Earth. Moreover, Barringer Crater and Tunguska's flattened forests are graphic reminders. They show that on random occasions such objects do produce horrific results. If the recent strikes and near misses are any indication, events that could kill thousands or even millions of people could happen several times per century. That means that the destructive potential of impact events for modern civilization is a good deal higher than most people realize.

Some Early Airblasts and Impacts

It is impossible to know how many large airblasts or impacts humans have witnessed over the millennia. At the time that an impactor created Barringer Crater, people existed on Earth but none of them had yet migrated into North America. So it is likely that the only witnesses to the event were animals.

Exactly when the first humans arrived in South America is still hotly debated. So it is unknown whether any people saw an unusual impact event that took place about

This chunk of rock, rich in nickel and iron, was found at the site of a meteorite impact. The metals indicate that the meteorite probably originated in the core of a failed planet.

10,000 years ago near what is now Rio Cuarto, in Argentina. Evidence shows that the impactor approached at a low angle, probably about 15 degrees. (Most impactors come in at 45 degrees or more.) It delivered a glancing blow. This created an elongated, oval-shaped crater with butterfly-shaped debris patterns along the edges. Yet despite this odd flight path, the object packed a wallop. It has been estimated that it exploded

Tektite is a type of glass-like rock; most scientists believe it is formed by the impact of meteorites on Earth's surface.

with a force some thirty times larger than the Tunguska blast, or more than a thousand Hiroshima bombs. If any people had been in the immediate area, they would have been killed instantly.

Another large impact that occurred more recently in human history demonstrates what happens when such an incident occurs in a densely populated region. The location was the province of Shanxi, in eastern China. According to Chinese chroniclers, in 1490 a huge explosion occurred in the sky, after which a terrifying rain of stones devastated the local towns and villages. At least 10,000 people died. Modern researchers think that a small asteroid disintegrated high in the atmosphere, producing millions of fragments. A similar but smaller and less destructive airblast occurred over western Germany in 1492. Because these events happened so long ago and were not investigated scientifically, nothing is known about the impactors themselves.

The Sikhote-Alin Event

A meteoric airblast that happened in 1947, over Russia, has been extensively investigated by trained scientists. Many believe it can be used as a fairly reliable model for events like those that took place in China and Germany in the 1490s. On February 12, 1947, the inhabitants of the Sikhote-Alin region of eastern Russia witnessed an enormous fireball high in the sky. Many people later testified that it was much brighter than the sun.

This initial explosion produced a swarm of smaller fireballs that shot across the sky at high speeds. They were accompanied by thunderous explosions and shock waves that shook buildings all across the area. According to one of the eyewitnesses, baker Korney Shvets:

> I saw blue flame sparkling in the sky because the meteorite was burning, and there were little fires trailing behind the main body. The windows of the bakery where I was working with my mother and brother trembled. A metal door of the oven flew open, and several hot charcoals fell out onto the floor. I was only 17 at the time, and I was scared because we thought it was an atomic bomb from the Americans. It was soon after the bomb fell on Hiroshima.

Scientists who examined the area soon afterward found 122 craters. The largest was 91 feet (28 m) across and 20 feet (6 m) deep. In the months and years that followed, the researchers recovered about 29 tons of meteorites from the craters and elsewhere in the region. They estimated that the impactor's original mass was in the range of 100 tons. Had it not broken up, the explosion

The Great 1492 Meteor

On November 7, 1492, a few weeks after Christopher Columbus's first landfall in the West Indies and about two years after the lethal rain of meteors in China, people in western Germany witnessed a startling event. An extremely bright fireball was seen high above the city of Basel. (The famous artist Albrecht Dürer witnessed it and painted it about a year later.) Soon after the fireball appeared, loud explosions issued from the sky and could be heard over an area of hundreds of square miles.

Another explosion occurred above the town of Ensisheim, and right afterward witnesses saw a large amount of dust and debris, including a large rock, fall to the ground. A big crowd gathered and dug up the stone, which weighed about 300 pounds (140 kg). This relic ended up in a succession of churches and museums, and a large piece of it survives today. The size of the original object that entered the atmosphere and exploded into countless shards is unknown. But there is little doubt that had it not broken apart, its impact could have flattened an entire German town.

generated by its impact could have easily wiped out a small town.

Too Close for Comfort

The seriousness of the threat posed by extraterrestrial impacts is further underscored by the large number of near misses. In many cases, both asteroids and comets have passed uncomfortably close to our planet. In 1770, Comet Lexell passed by Earth at a distance of about six

Peter Jenniskens, a meteor astronomer with NASA's Ames Research Center, approaches several meteorite fragments. They are among all that remains of an SUV-sized meteor that exploded in the sky over the desert of northern Sudan in October 2008. Scientists estimate that asteroids of that size (roughly 15 feet/4.6 meters in diameter) burn up in Earth's atmosphere approximately once each year.

times that of the moon, and many believe the object will return and make another pass at the planet about two hundred years from now. It is still too early to tell if it will miss Earth again or collide with it.

A much closer call, thankfully by a considerably smaller object, occurred in August 1972. The so-called "Great Daylight 1972 Fireball" was witnessed by tens of thousands of people in the American West. Entering the atmosphere above Utah, it passed within a mere 35 miles (57 km) of the ground before rushing back into space. The estimated size of the object was 46 feet (14 m) across, large enough, if it had hit, to demolish a moderate-sized town. A similar near miss by a relatively small object occurred at an altitude of 44 miles (71 km) above Japan in March 2006.

The consequences would have been far worse, however, if a near miss in 1989 had instead been a hit. In March of that year, an asteroid some 1,000 feet (300 m) across flew by the planet at a distance of only 400,000 miles; moreover, the object passed through the exact spot Earth had been in just six hours before. Had it not missed, it would have impacted either the land or sea with the force of thousands of Hiroshima bombs.

Impact in New Jersey

On April 23, 1922, the *New York Times* reported one of several dozen violent impact incidents that occurred in the United States during the twentieth century:

> A great ball of fire, trailing an iridescent tail like a comet, rushed across the sky near the southern New Jersey coast at 9 o'clock last night and disappeared earthward with an explosion that was heard over a thirty-mile area. . . . All [of the witnesses] insisted that the lightning-like illumination which accompanied its swift passage across the heavens and the terrific [huge] detonation with which it struck, rocking buildings and shattering windows, precluded [ruled out] it having been anything smaller than a heavenly [extraterrestrial] body. . . . The phenomenon lasted more than thirty seconds, in the course of which they [the witnesses] saw the fireball plunge earthward and felt it strike somewhere and rock the earth. The explosion they said was deafening.

NASA used computers to create this view of Earth as seen from the surface of the asteroid Toutatis. In 2004, this near-Earth object passed within a million miles (1.6 million km) of Earth.

Worse still would have been humanity's fate if an asteroid named Toutatis had struck Earth. About half the size of the K-T impactor, Toutatis passed within 960,000 miles (four times the moon's distance) of our planet in September 2004. It returned in 2008 and will continue to reappear every four years. Toutatis is one of a special class of objects that astronomers call near-Earth objects (NEOs). Evidence shows that they pose a far larger threat than ordinary asteroids and comets; the fate of the human race may one day rest in their fickle, hard-to-predict motions.

chapter Five

The Ongoing Danger of NEOs

This illustration shows a narrow asteroid belt filled with rocks and dusty debris orbiting a star. Asteroids are chunks of rocky material that, because of competing gravitational pulls, never managed to coalesce and form a planet. In our solar system, most asteroids circle in a belt between Mars and Jupiter.

ew potential extraterrestrial impactors can appear in Earth's vicinity at any time. An asteroid that has spent billions of years cruising the asteroid belt could suddenly break loose and head into the inner solar system. Or a comet long floating in the distant Oort Cloud could begin to fall inward toward the planets, including Earth. However, the threat posed to humanity by these scenarios is considerably less grim than the one posed by NEOs.

The asteroid Toutatis and numerous other asteroids and comets have orbits that carry them into the inner solar system—hence the name scientists assigned them: near-Earth objects. (They are sometimes called Earth-crossers for short.) NEOs "have crashed into the Earth in the past," one astronomer said while appraising the overall threat these bodies pose. "And their successors are potentially a threat to the Earth in the future. It is estimated that of the potential Earth-striking projectiles, about 90 percent are near-Earth asteroids or short-period comets."

Kinds and Numbers of Earth-crossers

Those NEOs that are asteroids are routinely referred to as NEAs, short for near-Earth asteroids. (They are also called earth-crossing asteroids, or ECAs.) For convenience, astronomers divide NEAs into groups according to the relationship between their orbits and Earth's orbit. Members of one of these groups, the Amores, for example, cross over Mars's orbit. They pass fairly close to Earth's orbit, although they do not actually cross it. Members of a second group of NEAs, the Apollos, do cross over Earth's orbit. Still another group of NEAs, the Atens, features objects that travel mainly inside Earth's orbit, which means that they are usually closer to the sun than Earth is.

The manner in which the NEAs and Earth-approaching comets manage to get into the inner solar system can be summed up in a single word—gravity. Asteroids orbiting in the asteroid belt are usually stable and remain in there. Similarly, most comets orbiting in the Oort Cloud tend to stay within that region of the outer solar system. However, now and then the gravities of the planets, especially that of the largest planet, Jupiter, interfere. A gravitational nudge

In 1996 the Near Earth Asteroid Rendezvous (NEAR) spacecraft was launched. It orbited a near-Earth asteroid known as Eros for more than a year, eventually landing safely on the surface. The NEAR spacecraft provided scientists with valuable data about the surface composition and physical properties of asteroids.

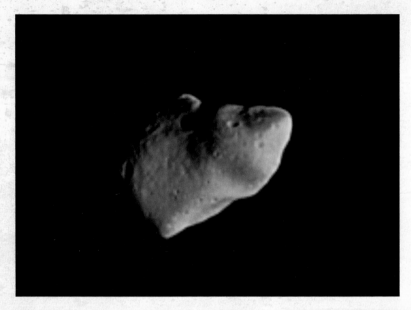

View of the large asteroid Gaspra, taken by the Galileo space-craft in 1991 from a distance of about 10,000 miles (16,000 km). Gaspra, which is located in the asteroid belt, is about 12 by 7.4 by 7 miles (19 by 12 by 11 km).

can cause an asteroid or comet to become unstable and migrate inward toward the sun. Eventually, such an object settles into a new orbit that periodically carries it close to one or more of the inner planets.

In accessing the threat posed by NEOs, the most important questions to answer are how big these bodies are and how many of them exist. Obviously, the bigger and more numerous they are, the larger the threat and vice-versa. At present, these questions regrettably cannot be answered with any confidence.

Only a few Earth-approaching comets are known. The largest, and the largest known NEO whose orbit crosses Earth's, is Comet Swift-Tuttle. The comet is 6.2 miles (10 km) wide, about the size of the K-T impactor. Calculations show that Swift-Tuttle will miss Earth on its next pass and

comet Swift-Tuttle's Discovery

Astronomer, geologist, and prolific science writer Patricia Barnes-Svarney penned this informative overview of how the largest NEO of all, Comet Swift-Tuttle, was found:

> In 1973, [noted astronomer Brian] Marsden had suggested that a comet seen in 1862 might be the same as reported by Ignatius Kegler, a Jesuit missionary, who observed the object in Beijing, China, in 1737. Marsden predicted the coincidence based on the idea that the jets [gaseous emissions] from the comet, once activated on its trip around the sun, could cause the comet slightly to change its orbit. If so, Marsden predicted the comet to arrive by the end of 1992, giving the comet a period of 130 years [to complete each circuit of its orbit]. The lost comet was found in the constellation of the Big Dipper on September 26, 1992, by Japanese amateur astronomer Tsuruhiko Kiuchi. Marsden was correct, although the date of the comet's closest approach to the sun was off by 17 days. . . . Marsden's orbital calculations [put] Comet Swift-Tuttle within several million miles from Earth in the year 3044. By then, we can only hope that humans will [have] developed an efficient method to eliminate such problems.

likely on many of its subsequent passes. But there is no guarantee that this trend will continue indefinitely. Over time, gravitational nudges by Jupiter and other planets could change the comet's orbit enough to bring about an eventual collision with Earth.

(Top) A technician tests instruments to be included in the Deep Impact space mission, 2005. The NASA spacecraft launched a three-foot by three-foot projectile into a comet, then gathered photos and data about the impact as well as the composition of the comet. (Inset) View from Deep Impact's probe taken 90 seconds before it hit the comet Tempel 1. The projectile created a crater on the comet's surface that was approximately 330 feet (100 meters) wide and 100 feet (30 meters) deep.

As for NEAs, so far roughly 170 have been identified, about half of them in the .6 mile (1 km) size range. However, scientists believe that the total number of these objects is much larger than those that have been spotted and recorded. The current consensus is that there are between 1,000 and 4,000 NEAs larger than .6 mile across; about 5,000 to 20,000 between 1,640 feet (500 m) and .6 miles across; approximately 150,000 to 1 million between 247 feet (100 m) and 1,640 feet across; and about 10 million to 1 billion between 25 feet (10 m) and 247 feet across.

Enormous Damage

These figures are sobering. Scientists agree that even a relatively small Earth-crosser could do enormous damage. The Tunguska object, for example, may well have been an NEA. An Earth-crosser may also have been responsible for a 1984 Pacific Ocean impact near Japan. Witnesses in a passing airliner saw an enormous explosion that produced a mushroom cloud that rose to a height of about 11 miles (18 km). The so-called Eastern Mediterranean Event, in June 2002, is another example. A likely NEA about 25 feet (10 m) across created an explosion the size of a small nuclear blast in the atmosphere between Greece and Libya.

Several recent close calls with confirmed NEAs provide further evidence of the seriousness of the threat these objects pose. If it had struck Earth, the asteroid that missed the planet by six hours in 1989 would have gouged out a crater 4.3 miles (7 km) in diameter. And the explosion would have released energy equivalent to that of more than sixty Hiroshima bombs.

The Menace of Icarus

Of Earth's recent near misses with NEOs, one of the more prominent was with asteroid 1566 Icarus. An Apollo asteroid, Icarus is about .9 miles (1.4 km) wide and will pass within 5 million miles of Earth in 2015. As Dwayne A. Day, a science writer for *Space Review*, pointed out, if this menacing object were to strike our planet sometime in the future, the results would be devastating:

> Icarus [periodically] swings by planet Earth, often coming within four million miles of the planet—mere spitting distance in astronomical terms. Icarus last passed by Earth in 1997. Before that, its previous approach was in June 1968. . . . [If it ever strikes our planet], the nearly mile wide chunk of rock would hit . . . with the force of 500,000 megatons—far larger than any major earthquake or volcanic eruption, and over thirty-three thousand times the size of the bomb that destroyed Hiroshima. At a minimum, it would kill millions, flattening buildings and trees for a radius of hundreds of miles, and/or causing huge [tsunamis] that would wipe out cities along thousands of miles of coastline. The dust it kicked into the atmosphere could even lead to a global winter lasting years.

Another near miss occurred on January 17, 1991. Asteroid 1991 BA, at about 30 feet (9 m) across, passed by Earth at less than a half of the Earth-moon distance. Another NEA, designated 1993 KA2, flew by our planet at about the same distance on May 20, 1993. This one was close to 36 feet (11 m) wide, making its potential impact large enough to annihilate a small town.

Considerably more dangerous as a potential impactor was the NEA called 2002 MN. It passed by Earth on June 14, 2002, missing it by 75,000 miles, about a third of the Earth-moon distance. It was one of the closest approaches of an asteroid or comet in modern times. With a width of 330 to 400 feet (100 to 120 m), it was at least twice the diameter of the Tunguska object and had several times its mass. So if it had come a little closer and struck an inhabited region of our planet, the consequences would have been dire. Depending on the population density of the area, from a few dozen to many millions of people could have perished. In addition, it should be pointed out that scientists did not know of the object's existence until *after* its close flyby. According to noted science writer Jeff Hecht:

> No one spotted asteroid 2002 MN until 17 June, three days after it sped by the Earth at 10.6 kilometers per second. The asteroid escaped earlier detection by approaching from the direction of the sun, which hid it from observation. It did enter the night sky when it passed the Earth, but initially was moving too fast to be picked up by automated survey cameras. Only when it was far enough from the Earth that it moved slowly across the stellar background did the MIT Lincoln Laboratory's LINEAR camera discover it. Despite their potential to cause local devastation, asteroids in the 50 to 100-meter range are receiving little attention. . . . One million of them may exist, but they are hard to protect against because they are too faint to see except when they are close to the Earth. [This] close encounter gave the Earth a reprieve from the perils of asteroid 2002 MN. It shifted the asteroid's 895-day orbit so it won't come close again until June 14, 2061.

This facility on Mount Bigelow, Arizona, contains one of three large telescopes scanning the skies for potentially dangerous objects. Astronomers with the Catalina Sky Survey—which also operates telescopes on Mount Lemmon, Arizona, and in Australia—are attempting to create an inventory of near-Earth objects, so that scientists can determine in advance how much of a threat each object presents to Earth.

A Recent Close Shave

A similar but even closer and more recent near-collision with an NEA occurred on March 2, 2009, when asteroid 2009 DD45 whizzed over the Pacific Ocean at a height of only 45,000 miles. Scientists estimate that if it had struck Earth it would have delivered a Tunguska-size blast. No trees would have been flattened in this case, however. As a water strike, it would have generated large tsunamis, which would have smashed into all the coastlines ringing the Pacific.

Because this asteroid did not impact Earth, no detailed estimates of the destruction it might have caused exist. However, some scientists have made educated guesses about possible large impacts in humanity's future. And the pictures they paint are not pretty.

chapter six

Future Threats of Large Impacts

If a large asteroid or comet strikes the Earth, human civilization could be wiped out by the resulting explosion, seismic activity, and other effects of the impact.

"Sorry. You have just been crushed by the shock wave, then vaporized by the heat of the [impacting] asteroid. You and every living thing around you for a thousand square kilometers or more are dead." This is one scientist's attempt to inject a little humor into the otherwise dismal prospect of a K-T-size object smashing into Earth sometime in the future.

It may be a long time—perhaps thousands or even millions of years—before an impactor that big strikes again. But sooner or later it will strike. Moreover, many other extraterrestrial objects, most smaller but a few larger than the dinosaur-killer, will collide with our planet. The fact is that the rain of cosmic debris evident in the remains of craters from past impacts is not over. It is merely that the human race is presently enjoying the relative peace and quiet that naturally exists between global catastrophes.

The major difference between past and future large impacts is that those in the future will be considerably more destructive and tragic than those in the past. To see why this is the case, one need only glance around at his or her surroundings. Today, the average person lives in a community of at least a few tens of thousands of people. Large numbers of people live in cities with populations of hundreds of thousands or millions. With some 340 cities having a million or more residents, Earth is far more densely populated than it was only a few hundred years ago. When one counts both human lives and the houses, bridges, ships, communities, and other countless products of human civilization, there is much more to lose today than there was when large impact events occurred in the past. Combining this fact with the certainty that such impacts will continue to happen must, at the least, give everyone pause.

Horrific Death Tolls

Human communities are so widely distributed across Earth's landmasses that even a fairly small impactor could be highly destructive. Consider, for instance, a rather common impact event—an airblast in which an incoming object explodes in the atmosphere. John S. Lewis has calculated what would happen if a 2.8 megaton airblast

A meteorite that strikes Earth near a population center such as Los Angeles would cause incredible loss of life.

occurred 10 miles (17 km) above an average city. The heat from the blast would ignite fires across an area 8 miles (13 km) across, he stated. In turn, this would likely create a firestorm similar to those that swept Tokyo, Dresden, and other cities that the United States carpet-bombed in World War II. Lewis estimates that this relatively moderate-size airblast would kill at least 8,000 people. That is nearly three times the death toll of the 9/11 terrorist attack in New York City.

Consider that the Tunguska blast, which was about five or six times larger than the one described above, killed mostly reindeer and other animals. That is because the 1908 event occurred in an area sparsely populated by humans. In grim comparison, if a

Tunguska-size impactor struck a populated sector of the United States today, the results would be horrific. If the region were rural, occupied mainly by small towns, somewhere between 60,000 and 70,000 people would die and property damages would be at least $4 billion. If the disaster happened in an urban area, it would cause some 300,000 deaths and upwards of $280 billion in property damages.

The Tunguska object was perhaps half the size of a football field and not capable of touching off a global catastrophe. What about an impactor .6 miles (1 km) across, the minimum size needed for such a catastrophe? Such a hunk of space rock would weigh about 1.5 billion tons, and it would carve out a crater 6 to 9 miles (10 to 15 km) wide. According to Duncan Steel, if the impact happened in Los Angeles, that city

> along with several kilometers of rock from the Earth's crust beneath it would be picked up and largely vaporized, lumps raining down on Hawaii and New York an hour or so later. Not that Honolulu or New York City would be left standing by then. Phenomenal seismic shocks [earthquakes] following the impact would have already shaken them flat.

Humanity on the Brink

As terrible as such a calamity sounds, it appears small beside the effects of potential strikes by even larger future impactors. An example would be an object 1.2 miles (2 km) across, twice as wide as the Los Angeles vaporizer. The larger impactor would produce an explosion not twice as big, but eight times as large as the smaller one.

Somewhere between 25 and 50 percent of the human race—1.5 to 3 billion people—would be exterminated.

The death toll would be especially large in so-called Third World countries. These nations possess less advanced food-growing capabilities and fewer large food stores than richer countries like the United States. So in the wake of the temporary breakdown in agriculture that would ensue in such a disaster, mass starvation would be much worse in poorer nations. Most of the agricultural destruction would result from the large amounts of dust the blast would throw into the atmosphere. The particles would absorb and block sunlight on a big enough scale to disrupt at least one or two growing seasons, leading to huge crop failures.

Worse still for humanity would be a strike by an asteroid or comet somewhat smaller than the K-T impactor. An object 4.8 miles (8 km) across, for instance, would have more than 500 times the mass of the Los Angeles vaporizer. As happened 65 million years ago, a gigantic fireball would expand outward from ground zero. Enormous shock waves, earthquakes, and tsunamis would be generated; fires would ignite across the globe; and an impact winter would cause a temporary breakdown of the food chain, along with mass extinctions. The human race itself would be on the brink of extinction. Some humans might well survive such a catastrophe, but they would number a few million (less than 1 percent of the former population) at best. And they would be plunged into stone-age conditions. The civilized standards and economic prosperity taken for granted today would take many centuries to rebuild.

Hollywood and Giant Impacts

Several big-budget Hollywood films have dealt with the threat of an extraterrestrial object wiping out humanity. Though dramatic, these cinematic impact scenarios have tended to be scientifically inaccurate. Astronomer Phil Plait pointed out some of the bad science in the popular 1998 blockbuster *Armageddon*, starring Bruce Willis:

> *Armageddon* got some astronomy right. For example, there is an asteroid in the movie, and asteroids do indeed exist. . . . Okay, so that was about all they got right. [For example] the [onscreen] director of NASA, Dan Truman, says that an asteroid "the size of Texas" was knocked out of the asteroid belt by a comet, which is why it is headed our way. . . . First off, there are no asteroids in the solar system that big. We'd have discovered them ages ago. Ceres, the largest asteroid in the main belt, is about 900 kilometers across, and Texas is about 1400 kilometers across. Even if we assume the size is an exaggeration, it still doesn't wash. A comet could not simply impact it and knock it out of orbit! An asteroid with a radius of, let's say, 500 kilometers and made of iron . . . would [weigh about] five million million million tons. That's a lot of asteroid. You could ram it with comets for years and not move it much. Plus, the odds of a comet hitting an asteroid at all are slim.

The Death of All Life

History clearly shows that even impactors packing the destructive power of the K-T killer are not close to the upper size limit for such objects. Remember that a small planet once smashed into Earth, creating the moon. Granted, the chances of something that enormous striking our planet again are slim. But there are plenty of objects far bigger than the K-T impactor that pose a credible future threat. An estimated three Earth-crossing objects in the 100-mile-wide (160-km-wide) size range move toward Earth every million years or so. Most of these will miss our planet. However, "if there are three of such size detected," Steel pointed out, "then it is safe to assume that there are dozens more awaiting discovery and, presumably, [numerous] smaller objects too faint to be detected with the telescopes presently being used."

Some of these potential Earth-smashers presently float between the giant planets Saturn and Uranus. Scientists call asteroids or comets orbiting among the outer planets "Centaurs." Charles Kowel, of the Mt. Palomar Observatory in California, discovered a particularly intriguing Centaur called Chiron in 1977. At first, scientists thought it was an asteroid. But in 1989, it developed a surrounding sheath of gases, suggesting it might be a comet.

Whatever Chiron is, its present orbit is unstable. Subject to periodic pushes and pulls by Saturn and Uranus, it could move into the inner solar system within a million years. Assuming humans still exist on Earth at that time, they could face a serious threat. Chiron may be as large as 143 miles (230 km) across. If it impacted Earth, it would create an immense basin-like depression in the range of a thousand miles wide. Such a colossal impact feature has been identified on Mercury. Called the Caloris

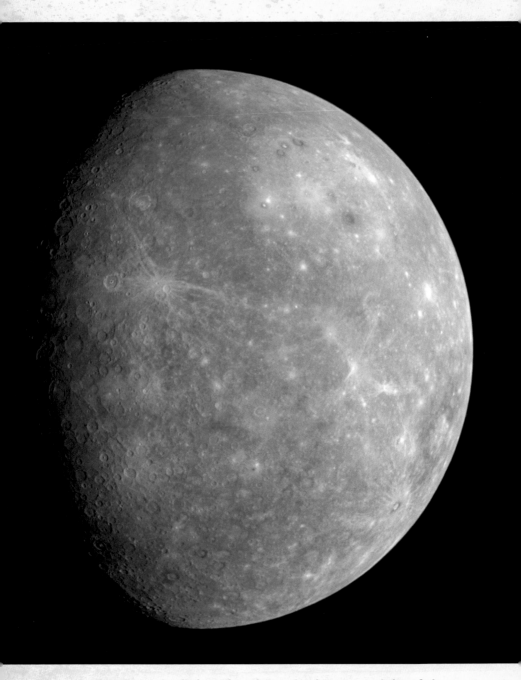

The large circular light-colored area in the upper right of the photograph of Mercury is the interior of the Caloris basin. This enormous feature—one of the largest impact basins in our solar system—may have been created about 3.8 billion years ago.

Basin, it is 960 miles (1,550 km) across. The formation of a similar basin on Earth would strip away a large portion of the planet's crust. Giant lava flows would erupt across Earth's surface; the air would become unbreathable; and all plant and animal life would die.

There is no doubt that in the future people will see such huge impactors coming. The question is whether they will be able to save humanity from extinction. And the answer might be yes, as scientists already have begun to search for ways to stop threatening space objects.

chapter seven

Confronting the Threat from Space

The Kitt Peak National Observatory near Tuscon, Arizona, hosted the first effort to find near-Earth asteroids during the 1980s.

That humanity lives under the real threat
of destruction from large extraterrestrial
impact events has been established
beyond the shadow of a doubt. "We are perpetually poised on the edge of extinction," Gerrit
Verschuur asserted. He then asked, "Now that
we have learned the truth, what will our species
do with this knowledge?" Verschuur answered
this question by advocating the construction of a
"planetary defense system."

Some people are surprised to find that the
concept of confronting and dealing with impact
threats from space is not new, even predating

the twentieth century. In 1822, famous English poet and intellectual Lord Byron, who recognized such threats in his writings, stated:

> Who knows whether, when a comet shall approach this globe to destroy it, as it often has been and will be destroyed, men will not tear rocks from their foundations by means of steam, and hurl mountains, as the giants are said to have done, against the flaming mass? And then we shall have traditions of Titans [early Greek gods of giant stature] again, and of wars with Heaven.

The first modern scientists to propose a concerted effort to counter the impact menace were Allan O. Kelly and Frank Dachille. In their 1953 book *Target Earth*, they wrote that it was necessary to engage in

> perpetual surveillance of a critical envelope of space with the charting of all objects that come close to a collision course with the Earth. It will require, further, that on discovery of a dangerous object [that certain] moves be made to protect the Earth.

Some have argued that close studies and updated catalogues of possible impactors are needed to help differentiate between them and nuclear explosions. They point out the case of an ominous incident that occurred in 1994. A meteoric airblast having the power of almost twenty Hiroshima bombs occurred over the Pacific Ocean. President Bill Clinton's advisers awakened him because they were at first worried that a foreign country might have set off a nuclear device. Finding as many existing Earth-crossers as possible is essential, said Steel, "lest an ill-timed and ill-placed natural event mistakenly provokes a nuclear war."

Searching for NEOs

The first systematic scientific effort to search for and calcu-late the paths of potential Earth impactors began in 1972. That year Eugene Shoemaker and a colleague, Eleanor

An aerospace engineer uses a twelve-inch reflecting telescope to observe asteroids from Schriever Air Force Base in Colorado. The Lincoln Near-Earth Asteroid Research (LINEAR) project is a cooperative effort that involves the U.S. Air Force, NASA, and the Lincoln Laboratory at the Massachusetts Institute of Technology (MIT).

Scanning the Skies

Among the scientific programs currently looking for and cataloguing NEOs is the Catalina Sky Survey (CSS), run by Stephen M. Larson for the University of Arizona. The CSS distinguished itself by discovering some 70 percent of all the NEOs found between 2006 and 2009. The following is part of the CSS's mission statement:

> The mission of the Catalina Sky Survey is to contribute to the inventory of near-earth objects (NEOs), or more specifically, the potentially hazardous asteroids (PHAs) that pose an impact risk to Earth and its inhabitants. . . . Given the catastrophic consequences of a collision [of Earth] with a large object, it would be irresponsible not to carry out an inventory now. The NEO Observations Program (NEOO) is a result of a 1998 congressional directive to NASA to conduct a program to identify 1 km. or larger bodies to an estimated 90 percent confidence level or better. Since then a further mandate (June, 2006) has been issued to identify 140 meter or larger bodies to the same confidence level. . . . These surveys are operated in such a manner that same night follow up on newly discovered objects can usually be done facilitating the rapid determination of orbits and thus the specific hazard posed by the newly found objects.

Helin, initiated the Planet-Crossing Asteroid Survey (PCAS). Using one of the smaller telescopes at Mt. Palomar, this two-person team more than doubled the number of known Earth-crossers by the late 1970s. Shoemaker realized that Earth-crossers were not the only objects that posed a threat. So in 1982 he, his wife Carolyn, and fellow scientist David Levy began cataloguing asteroids and comets in the outer solar system. The new program became known as the Palomar Asteroid and Comet Survey (PACS).

Other searches for potentially dangerous space objects soon followed. One, set up by Duncan Steel in 1989, was the Anglo-Australian Near-Earth Asteroid Survey (AANEAS). Another was the Spacewatch program. It was established at Kitt Peak Observatory (in Arizona) in the 1980s by astronomer Tom Gehrels.

In the early 1990s the U.S. Congress asked some NASA scientists to look into setting up a program for identifying large Earth-approaching objects. The congressional panel called on the researchers to "define a program for dramatically increasing the detection rate of Earth-orbit-crossing asteroids," and to "define systems and technologies to alter the orbits of such asteroids or to destroy them if they should pose a danger of life on Earth." The result was the Spaceguard Survey, a loose collection of groups, scientists, and telescopes around the world tasked with finding possible Earth impactors.

In spite of these earnest and impressive efforts to find possible Earth impactors, scientists generally agree that more needs to be done. Simply put, enormous numbers of these objects are hurtling through the solar system, and finding them all will require many more telescopes and researchers. NASA physicist David Morrison has pointed out that the total number of scientists in the world presently searching for potential impactors is fewer than the number of people who work in a typical McDonald's restaurant.

Various Deflection Strategies

Finding potentially lethal NEOs is, of course, only part of the task of reducing the impact threat. If one of the search groups does find a large asteroid or comet on a collision course with Earth, the next obvious step is to try to stop the impactor.

Most scientists agree that the best approach is to deflect a threatening object–that is, to change its orbit so that it misses rather than strikes Earth. Ideally, they say, this

A rocket meant to carry a nuclear warhead is launched from Vandenberg Air Force Base in California. Even the largest nuclear weapons in existence today might not be powerful enough to destroy an incoming asteroid or deflect it from a collision course with the Earth.

should be done when the object is as far away as possible. That way, an initially small orbital change would have time to add up to a larger one by the time the object reaches our planet's vicinity. "Early detection," one scientist has pointed out, "gives a much longer reaction time. More importantly, interceptions far from Earth—made feasible by early warning—are much more desirable and easier than interceptions near Earth."

The other extreme—waiting until only a few weeks or days are left before impact—would be disastrous, scientists say. In such a case, Gerrit Verschuur quipped, "nothing could be done except duck." He added, wryly:

At such times the entrances to caves might become prime real estate, although there would be little to guarantee one's safety once inside, given that violent earthquakes following a severe impact might cause them to collapse.

The most effective way to deflect an oncoming space object remains uncertain. The immediate gut reaction for many people is to blow up the impactor, hopefully eliminating it. This is the approach seen most often in movies about impact threats, such as *Deep Impact* and *Armageddon* (both 1998). In such a scenario, a rocket carries a nuclear device to the onrushing object and detonates it either on or beneath its surface.

This approach has some major inherent problems, however. First, if the object is large and composed mostly of hard materials like iron, even the largest nuclear weapons that humans possess will not be powerful enough to do the job. Second, even if the explosion does shatter the impactor, the fragments will remain on the same collision course. And the threat might well be worse than before. "The resulting rain of fairly large-size chunks of rock could have more globally devastating consequences than the strike of the original asteroid," Barnes-Svarney stated. "If the chunks were large and spread out enough, their searing heat could spark massive firestorms around the world."

Among the other suggested ways of deflecting an oncoming impactor is to attach a thin but wide "solar sail" to the object. The solar wind (streams of particles emitted by the sun) hopefully would push on the sail, dragging the impactor off its course. Still another approach would be to place robots and a gun-like device on the object's surface. The robots would gather pieces of the impactor, and the gun would fire them away into space, reducing the object's mass and pushing it into a new orbit. More promising than these approaches, most scientists agree, would be a "stand-off" explosion. A rocket would carry a nuke close to, but not onto, the impactor. Hopefully, the blast would be strong enough to nudge the object off-course without fragmenting it into multiple impactors.

The Key to Human Survival

It is possible that one or more of these approaches will work with small or moderate size impactors. For the time being, however, the general consensus is that humanity will not be able to stop an oncoming object large enough to bring about a global catastrophe. The great Eugene Shoemaker aptly summed it up shortly before his untimely death (in a car accident) in 1997. Even with all the impressive discoveries and feats it has made in the past century, he said, modern science must face the realization

Earth as an Alien Planet

Most scientists say that if a large extraterrestrial object threatens Earth in the near future, nothing could be done to stop it. The only way to save humanity from extinction would be to load a few hundred, or at best a few thousand, people into space shuttles and similar craft and get them off the planet before the collision occurs. That way enough humans would survive to perpetuate the species. The main problem in such a scenario, as Gerrit Verschuur stated, is the bleak world the escapees would face when they returned after the disaster:

> Who will welcome them back upon their return? Where would they land? If we could afford to set up colonies on the moon or Mars, the colonists could wait until after the dust had settled before attempting to return. The problem with this option is that, after a really healthy thwack, the Earth's environment would be so altered that returning human beings might find this to be an alien planet.

"that humankind is not yet ready to defend Earth against asteroidal or cometary impact."

Yet like many of his colleagues, Shoemaker was optimistic about the future. He believed that, given enough time, diligent researchers will develop and perfect the technologies and methods needed to keep our planet safe from impact catastrophes. For human beings, he stated, the key to success and ultimate survival, will be "continuous study." Scientists across the world must seek and

To ensure that humans would survive an impact event, some small proportion of the population might have to be launched into space, where they would escape the devastation that an impact would cause on Earth.

obtain the necessary funding from their respective governments and use it in sustained, concerted efforts to make sure humanity does have a future. The sober fact, Shoemaker said, is that deadly giant space rocks "may appear at any time from any direction." And "exploratory research and constant surveillance of the skies must be our answer to the threat of impact."

c. 4.5 billion B.C.: Earth forms from the steady accumulation of dust, rocks, and other debris orbiting the infant sun.

c. 4.5 billion B.C.: An object the size of Mars smashes into Earth, sending large amounts of debris into orbit; these materials coalesce, forming the moon.

c. 212 million B.C.: A huge impact event creates the Manicouagan Crater in Canada.

c. 65 million B.C.: An asteroid impact known as the K-T event occurs, causing a mass extinction that includes the demise of the dinosaurs.

c. 50,000 B.C.: An asteroid impact creates Barringer Crater in Arizona.

c. 12,900 B.C.: An impact event centered in southern Canada contributes to the extinction of large mammals, including woolly mammoths.

A.D. 1490: More than 10,000 people die in an asteroid impact in China.

1694: English astronomer Edmund Halley suggests that the biblical great flood was caused by a comet impact.

1822: The famous English poet Lord Byron proposes the idea of destroying deadly incoming space objects.

1908: An impactor explodes in the atmosphere above the Tunguska River, in Siberia, producing a huge fireball and flattening entire forests.

1927: Soviet scientists first begin direct studies of the Tunguska blast.

1945: An airblast of a meteor over Pennsylvania shakes houses and rattles windows.

1947:   An impactor creates an enormous fireball and 122 craters in eastern Russia.

1949:   American scientist Ralph Baldwin asserts that most lunar craters were caused by impacts.

1972:   A giant fireball is seen across the American West as a large meteor passes through Earth's atmosphere. Eugene Shoemaker, a noted planetary scientist and pioneering expert on extraterrestrial impacts, establishes the Planet-Crossing Asteroid Survey (PCAS).

1977:   Chiron, a large asteroid or comet, is discovered in an unstable orbit near the planet Saturn.

1994:   The fragments of Comet Shoemaker-Levy 9 crash into Jupiter, creating explosions the size of Earth.

1998:   Two popular Hollywood films about extraterrestrial impact—*Armageddon* and *Deep Impact*—are released.

2002:   An asteroid about 25 feet across explodes in the atmosphere between Greece and Libya.

2004:   The large asteroid Toutatis passes within 960,000 miles of Earth.

2009:   Asteroid 2009 DD45 passes over the Pacific Ocean at a height of only 45,000 miles.

Chapter 1: The Day the Sky Exploded

p. 8: "If it had struck . . ." Andrew Alden, "Tunguska: The Cosmic Hit of the Century," http://geology.about.com/od/impacts/a/tunguska.htm.

p. 9: "Early in the morning . . ." Quoted in William K. Hartmann, "1908 Siberia Explosion: Reconstructing an Asteroid Impact from Eyewitness Accounts," http://www.psi.edu/projects/siberia/siberia.html.

p. 10: "I was sitting on the porch . . ." Ibid.

p. 10: "I saw the sky in the north open . . ." Ibid.

p. 11: "The whirlwind knocked the *dyukcha* . . ." "The Tunguska Event: Eyewitness Account of Akulina Lyuchetkana, on the Dilyushmo River," http://www.vurdalak.com/tunguska/witness/lyuchetkana_a.htm.

p. 17: "Because the meteor did not strike . . ." Hartmann, "1908 Siberia Explosion."

p. 18: "The seabed is cracked . . ." John S. Lewis, *Rain of Iron and Ice: The Real Threat of Comet and Asteroid Bombardment* (Reading, MA: Addison-Wesley, 1996), 151.

Chapter 2: Evidence for Deadly Impacts

p. 22: "If people reacted to the impact threat . . ." Duncan Steel, *Rogue Asteroids and Doomsday Comets* (New York: John Wiley, 1997), 53.

p. 22: "All of the people in the room . . ." Ibid, 23-24.

p. 24: "At great distances from the sun . . ." Patricia Barnes-Svarney, *Asteroid: Earth Destroyer or New Frontier?* (New York: Plenum, 1996), 118-119.

p. 26: "the result of a long game . . ." David H. Levy, *Comets: Creators and Destroyers* (New York: Simon and Schuster, 1998), 25.

p. 29: "The explosion that caused the crater Tycho . . ." Quoted in Steel, *Rogue Asteroids and Doomsday Comets*, 21-22.

p. 29: "We can now regard as completely unfounded . . ." Quoted in Curtis Peebles, *Asteroids: A History* (Washington, DC: Smithsonian Institution, 2000), 159.

p. 31: "When a sizable solid body . . ." Eugene M. Shoemaker and Carolyn S. Shoemaker, "The Role of Collisions," in J. Kelly Beatty et al, *The New Solar System* (Cambridge, Eng.: Cambridge University Press, 1999), 70.

p. 31: "The impacting body was as bright . . ." Barnes-Svarney, *Asteroid*, 153-154.

p. 37: "The explosions of the larger bodies . . ." Lewis, *Rain of Iron and Ice*, 148-149.

Chapter 3: Giant Impacts and Mass Extinctions

p. 39: "We need to consider the story . . ." Quoted in Steel, *Rogue Asteroids and Doomsday Comets*, 94.

p. 41: "Seeming to swell in size . . ." Neil F. Comins, *What if the Moon Didn't Exist? Voyages to Earths that Might Have Been* (New York: HarperCollins, 1993), 3.

p. 42: "Life could have been killed off . . ." Barnes-Svarney, *Asteroid*, 208.

p. 47: "Following the impact . . ." Gerrit L. Verschuur, *Impact: The Threat of Comets and Asteroids* (New York: Oxford University Press, 1996), 11.

p. 48: "After the dinosaurs were ushered off . . ." Ibid., 7-8.

p. 50: "The destruction would have been instantaneous . . ." Quoted in Linda M. Howe, "Nanodiamonds Link Outer Space Impactors to Earth Extinctions 12,900 Years Ago," http://www.earthfiles.com/news.php?ID=1517&category= Science.

Chapter 4: Recent Strikes and Near Misses

p. 53: "Hundreds of thousands of persons . . ." Quoted in Lewis, *Rain of Iron and Ice*, 129.

p. 56: "I saw blue flame sparkling . . ." Quoted in Roy Gallant, "Sikhote-Alin Revisited," http://web.archive.org/web/20010415042416/http://www.meteor.co.nz/feb96_1.html.

p. 59: "A great ball of fire . . ." Quoted in Lewis, *Rain of Iron and Ice*, 126.

Chapter 5: The Ongoing Danger of NEOs

p. 64: "have crashed into the Earth . . ." Barnes-Svarney, *Asteroid*, 211.

p. 67: "In 1973, [noted astronomer Brian] Marsden . . ." Ibid., 219-220.

p. 70: "Icarus [periodically] swings by . . ." Dwayne A. Day, "Giant Bombs on Giant Rockets: Project Icarus," http://www.thespacereview.com/article/175/1.

p. 71: "No one spotted asteroid 2002 MN . . ." Jeff Hecht, "Asteroid's Near-miss with Earth," http://www.newscientist.com/article/dn2444.

Chapter 6: Future Threats of large Impacts

p. 75: "Sorry. You have just been crushed . . ." Barnes-Svarney, *Asteroid*, 223.

p. 78: "along with several kilometers of rock . . ." Steel, *Rogue Asteroids and Doomsday Comets*, 1.

p. 80: "Armageddon got some astronomy right . . ." Phil Plait, "The Astronomy of Armageddon," http://www.badastronomy.com/bad/movies/armpitageddon.html.

p. 81: "if there are three of such size detected . . ." Steel, *Rogue Asteroids and Doomsday Comets*, 127.

Chapter 7: Confronting the Threat from Space

p. 85: "We are perpetually poised . . ." Verschuur, *Impact*, 220.

p. 86: "Who knows whether . . ." Quoted in NASA, "Early Ideas About Impacts and Extinctions," http://impact.arc.nasa.gov/news_detail.cfm?ID=72.

p. 86, "perpetual surveillance of a critical envelope . . ." Ibid.

p. 86: "lest an ill-timed . . ." Steel, *Rogue Asteroids and Doomsday Comets*, 204.

p. 88: "The mission of the Catalina Sky Survey . . ." "Catalina Sky Survey Mission," http://www.lpl.arizona.edu/css/css_mission.html.

p. 89: "define a program . . ." Quoted in "Spaceguard Survey," http://impact.arc.nasa.gov/downloads/spacesurvey.pdf.

p. 91: "Early detection . . ." Peebles, *Asteroids*, 226.

p. 91: "nothing could be done except duck . . ." Verschuur, *Impact*, 206.

p. 92: "The resulting rain . . ." Barnes-Svarney, *Asteroid*, 257-258.

p. 93: "Who will welcome them back . . ." Verschuur, *Impact*, 204.

p. 93: "that humankind is not yet ready . . ." Shoemaker, "The Role of Collisions," in *The New Solar System*, 85.

p. 93: "continuous study . . ." Ibid.

airblast: The explosion of an incoming asteroid or comet in the atmosphere.

antimatter: An alternate, exotic, and rare form of matter proposed by scientists; in theory, mixing matter and antimatter would produce a violent explosion and release of energy.

asteroid: A small stony or metallic body orbiting the sun, most often (though not always) in the asteroid belt.

asteroid belt: A region lying between the orbits of Mars and Jupiter, where most asteroids are located.

comet: A body consisting of rocks, dust, and various kinds of ices that orbits the sun, often (though not always) in the Oort Cloud.

crust: Earth's outermost layer.

detonation: An explosion.

extinct: Dead; the term usually refers to the death of a species.

extraterrestrial: Originating or occurring beyond Earth.

impact crater: A hole in the ground created by the crash of an asteroid or comet from space.

impact event: The collision of an asteroid, comet, or other space object with Earth or another heavenly body.

impactor: An object that strikes Earth or another heavenly body.

impact winter: A period of darkened skies and cooler temperatures caused by dust injected into the atmosphere by a large impact event.

K-T event: The catastrophe that caused a mass extinction of plant and animal species, including the dinosaurs, about 65 million years ago as a result of the impact of a large comet or asteroid.

Glossary

lunar: Having to do with the moon.

mass: The total amount of matter contained in an object.

megafauna: Woolly mammoths, giant sloths, and other large mammals that became extinct several thousands years ago.

meteor (or meteoroid): A small piece of space debris.

meteorite: A meteor that survives a fall through Earth's atmosphere.

near-Earth asteroids (NEAs): Asteroids that come near or cross Earth's orbit.

near-Earth objects (NEOs): Asteroids, comets, or other space objects that come near or cross Earth's orbit.

Oort Cloud: A vast shell of comets located in the solar system's outer reaches.

orbit: To move around something; most commonly refers to the path taken by a planet, comet, or asteroid around the sun as well as a moon around a planet.

photosynthesis: The natural process by which plants absorb carbon dioxide and release oxygen.

planetesimals: Solid objects that orbited the infant sun and coalesced to form the planets and their moons; some planetesimals survived as asteroids and comets.

solar: Having to do with the sun.

solar system: The sun and all the planets, moons, and other objects orbiting it.

species: An individual kind of plant or animal.

terrestrial: On or having to do with Earth.

tsunami: A giant sea wave generated by an earthquake, landslide, volcanic eruption, or extraterrestrial impact.

universe: Everything known to exist.

Selected Books and Articles

Alvarez, Louis W. and Walter Alvarez, et al. "Extraterrestrial Cause for the Cretaceous-Tertiary Extinction," *Science*, vol. 208, 1980.

Alvarez, Walter. *T. Rex and the Crater of Doom.* Princeton, NJ: Princeton University Press, 1997.

Azimov, Isaac. *A Choice of Catastrophes.* New York: Simon and Schuster, 1979.

Barnes-Svarney, Patricia. *Asteroid: Earth Destroyer or New Frontier?* New York: Plenum, 1996.

Beatty, J. Kelly, et al. *The New Solar System.* Cambridge, Eng.: Cambridge University Press, 1999.

Chapman, Clark R. and David Morrison. *Cosmic Catastrophes.* New York: Plenum, 1989.

———. "Impacts on Earth by Asteroids and Comets: Assessing the Hazard," *Nature*, vol. 367, 1994.

Comins, Neil F. *What if the Moon Didn't Exist? Voyages to Earths that Might Have Been.* New York: HarperCollins, 1993.

Gehrels, Tom, ed. *Hazards Due to Comets and Asteroids.* Tucson: University of Arizona Press, 1994.

Glenn, William, ed. *The Mass Extinction Debates: How Science Works in a Crisis.* Stanford, CA: Stanford University Press, 1994.

Levy, David H. *Comets: Creators and Destroyers.* New York: Simon and Schuster, 1998.

Levy, David H. and Eugene M. Shoemaker, et al. "Comet Shoemaker-Levy 9 Meets Jupiter," *Scientific American*, vol. 273, 1995.

Lewis, John S. *Rain of Iron and Ice: The Real Threat of Comet and Asteroid Bombardment.* Reading, MA: Addison-Wesley, 1996.

Morrison, David. "Target Earth," *Astronomy*, February 2002.

Paul, Gregory S., ed. *The Scientific American Book of Dinosaurs.* New York: St. Martin's Press, 2000.

Bibliography

Peebles, Curtis. *Asteroids: A History.* Washington, DC: Smithsonian Institution, 2000.

Powell, James L. *Night Comes to the Cretaceous: Comets, Craters, Controversy, and the Last Days of the Dinosaurs.* New York: Harcourt Brace, 1998.

Rothery, David A. *Volcanoes, Earthquakes, and Tsunamis.* London: Hodder, 2007.

Rubin, Alan E. *Disturbing the Solar System: Impacts, Close Encounters, and Coming Attractions.* Princeton, NJ: Princeton University Press, 2002.

Steel, Duncan. *Rogue Asteroids and Doomsday Comets.* New York: John Wiley, 1997.

Verschuur, Gerrit L. *Impact: The Threat of Comets and Asteroids.* New York: Oxford University Press, 1996.

The Atlantic, "The Sky is Falling"

http://www.theatlantic.com/doc/200806/asteroids

Catalina Star Survey

http://www.lpl.arizona.edu/css/

NASA, "Asteroids"

http://nssdc.gsfc.nasa.gov/planetary/text/asteroids.txt

NASA, "Facts About NEO Impacts"

http://impact.arc.nasa.gov/intro_faq.cfm

The Observer,
"UN is Told that Earth Needs an Asteroid Shield"

http://www.guardian.co.uk/science/2008/dec/07/
space-technology-asteroid-shield

Science Daily, "Extraterrestrial Impact
Likely Source Of Sudden Ice Age Extinctions"

http://www.sciencedaily.com/releases/2007/09/
070924172959.htm

Science News,
"Did Asteroid Cause Ancient N.Y. Tsunami?"

http://dsc.disco.com/news/2008/11/20/
asteroid-tsunami.html

web sites

Smithsonian Astrophysical Observatory,
One-mile-wide Asteroid to Pass Close to the Earth in 2028"

http://cfa-www.harvard.edu/iau/pressinfo/1997XF11.html

Index

Numbers in **bold italics** refer to captions.

Picture credits

2: Courtesy Phillipp Salzgeber (http://salzgeber.at/astro/pics/9703293.html)

6-7: Used under license from Shutterstock, Inc.

9: © OTTN Publishing

12: The Leonid Kulik Expedition/NASA

15: U.S. Air Force Photo/DoD

18: Otis Imboden/National Geographic/Getty Images

20-21: Used under license from Shutterstock, Inc.

23: NASA Kennedy Space Center (NASA-KSC)

25: NASA Jet Propulsion Laboratory (NASA-JPL)

28: NASA Jet Propulsion Laboratory (NASA-JPL)

30: NASA Headquarters - Greatest Images of NASA (NASA-HQ-GRIN)

32: Used under license from Shutterstock, Inc.

33: NASA

34: NASA Jet Propulsion Laboratory (NASA-JPL)

35: NASA/JPL/Space Science Institute

36: (top)NASA Jet Propulsion Laboratory (NASA-JPL); (bottom) NASA/JPL/Infrared Telescope Facility

40: Used under license from Shutterstock, Inc.

42: NASA/David Scott

43: Used under license from Shutterstock, Inc.

45: NASA Langley Research Center (NASA-LaRC)

46: Dennis Josefczyk/Alaska Volcano Observatory

49: Used under license from Shutterstock, Inc.

52: Katsuhiro Mouri and Shuji Kobayashi (Nagoya City Science Museum and Planetarium)/NASA

54: Used under license from Shutterstock, Inc.

55: Used under license from Shutterstock, Inc.

58: NASA Ames Research Center/SETI/Peter Jenniskens

60: NASA Jet Propulsion Laboratory (NASA-JPL)

62-63: NASA/JPL-Caltech/T. Pyle (SSC)

65: NASA Marshall Space Flight Center (NASA-MSFC)

66: NASA Jet Propulsion Laboratory (NASA-JPL)

68: (top) NASA Kennedy Space Center (NASA-KSC); (inset) SA/JPL-Caltech/UMD

72: NASA/CSS

74-75:Used under license from Shutterstock, Inc.

77: Used under license from Shutterstock, Inc.

82: NASA Jet Propulsion Laboratory (NASA-JPL)

84-85: Used under license from Shutterstock, Inc.

87: U.S. Air Force Photo/DoD

90: F. J. Hooker/DoD

94: NASA/Sandra Joseph-Kevin O'Connell

Cover:Used under license from Shutterstock, Inc.